MW01470737

I LOVE YOU, MOM

And Here's Why...

Text copyright © 2024 by Familius
Illustration copyright © 2024 by Olivia Herrick
All rights reserved.

Published by Familius LLC, www.familius.com
PO Box 1130, Sanger, CA 93657

Familius books are available at special discounts for bulk purchases, whether for sales promotions or for family or corporate use. For more information, contact Familius Sales at orders@familius.com.

Reproduction of this book in any manner, in whole or in part, without written permission of the publisher is prohibited.

Library of Congress Control Number: 2024940344

Print ISBN 9781641708968
Ebook ISBN 9798893960310

Printed in China

Edited by Brooke Jorden
Cover and book design by Olivia Herrick

10 9 8 7 6 5 4 3 2 1

First Edition

MOTHERHOOD

AND

RELATIONSHIPS

There is no friendship, no love, like that of a mother for her child.

HENRY WARD BEECHER

AMERICAN CLERGYMAN AND SOCIAL REFORMER

We are born of love; love is our mother.

RUMI
13TH-CENTURY
PERSIAN POET

Motherhood: All love begins and ends there.

ROBERT BROWNING

ENGLISH POET AND PLAYWRIGHT

MOTHER'S LOVE IS PEACE.
IT NEED NOT BE ACQUIRED;
IT NEED NOT BE DESERVED.

ERICH FROMM

GERMAN SOCIAL PSYCHOLOGIST

A MOTHER'S ARMS ARE MORE COMFORTING THAN ANYONE ELSE'S.

DIANA

PRINCESS OF WALES

THE MOMENT A CHILD IS BORN, THE MOTHER IS ALSO BORN. SHE NEVER EXISTED BEFORE. THE WOMAN EXISTED, BUT THE MOTHER, NEVER. A MOTHER IS SOMETHING ABSOLUTELY NEW.

RAJNEESH
INDIAN GURU AND SPIRITUAL TEACHER

A mother is your first friend, your best friend, your forever friend.

UNKNOWN

A mother is not a person to lean on, but a person to make leaning unnecessary.

DOROTHY C. FISHER

AMERICAN AUTHOR AND SOCIAL ACTIVIST

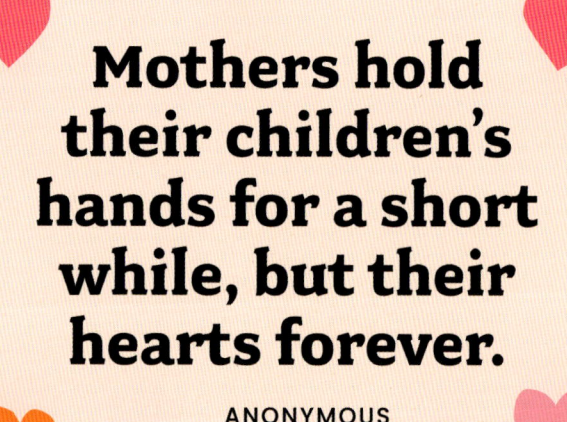

Mothers hold their children's hands for a short while, but their hearts forever.

ANONYMOUS

Mothers are like glue.

Even when you can't see them, they're still holding the family together.

SUSAN GALE
AUTHOR

THE MOTHER-CHILD RELATIONSHIP IS PARADOXICAL AND, IN A SENSE, TRAGIC.

IT REQUIRES THE MOST INTENSE LOVE ON THE MOTHER'S SIDE,

YET THIS VERY LOVE MUST HELP THE CHILD GROW AWAY FROM THE MOTHER,

AND TO BECOME FULLY INDEPENDENT.

ERICH FROMM
GERMAN SOCIAL PSYCHOLOGIST

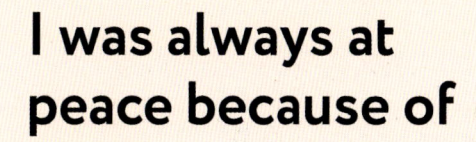

I was always at peace because of the way my mom treated me.

MARTINA HINGIS
SWISS PROFESSIONAL TENNIS PLAYER

A mother's arms are made of tenderness, and children sleep soundly in them.

VICTOR HUGO

FRENCH NOVELIST AND POET

A MAN NEVER SEES ALL THAT HIS MOTHER HAS BEEN TO HIM UNTIL IT'S TOO LATE TO LET HER KNOW HE SEES IT.

WILLIAM DEAN HOWELLS
AMERICAN AUTHOR AND LITERARY CRITIC

ONCE YOU'RE A MOM, YOU'RE ALWAYS A MOM. IT'S LIKE RIDING A BIKE, YOU NEVER FORGET.

TARAJI P. HENSON

AMERICAN ACTRESS AND SINGER

No language can express the power, and beauty, and heroism, and majesty of a mother's love. It shrinks not where man cowers, and grows stronger where man faints, and over wastes of worldly fortunes sends the radiance of its quenchless fidelity like a star.

EDWIN HUBBELL CHAPIN
AMERICAN PREACHER AND EDITOR

The tie which links mother and child is of such pure and immaculate strength as to be never violated.

WASHINGTON IRVING

AMERICAN AUTHOR AND HISTORIAN

MOST OF ALL THE OTHER BEAUTIFUL THINGS IN LIFE COME BY TWOS AND THREES, BY DOZENS AND HUNDREDS. PLENTY OF ROSES, STARS, SUNSETS, RAINBOWS, BROTHERS, AND SISTERS, AUNTS AND COUSINS, BUT ONLY ONE MOTHER IN THE WHOLE WORLD.

KATE DOUGLAS WIGGIN
AMERICAN AUTHOR AND EDUCATOR

ATTITUDE

The fastest way to break the cycle of perfectionism and become a fearless mother is to give up the idea of doing it perfectly—indeed, to embrace uncertainty and imperfection.

ARIANNA HUFFINGTON
GREEK-AMERICAN AUTHOR AND COLUMNIST

There is no way to be a perfect mother,

and a million ways

to be a good one.

JILL CHURCHILL
AMERICAN AUTHOR

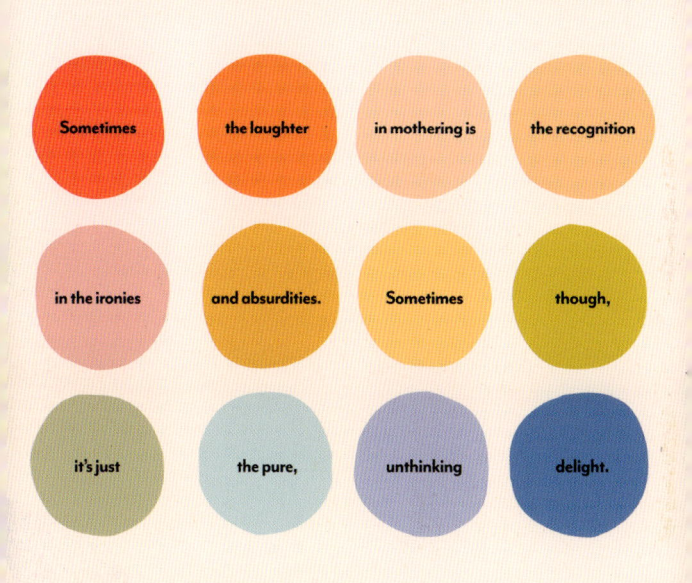

Sometimes the laughter in mothering is the recognition in the ironies and absurdities. Sometimes though, it's just the pure, unthinking delight.

BARBARA SCHAPIRO

AMERICAN AUTHOR AND PROFESSOR

IT'S UP TO US, AS MOTHERS AND MOTHER-FIGURES, TO GIVE THE GIRLS IN OUR LIVES THE KIND OF SUPPORT THAT KEEPS THEIR FLAME LIT AND LIFTS UP THEIR VOICES—NOT NECESSARILY WITH OUR OWN WORDS, BUT BY LETTING THEM FIND THE WORDS THEMSELVES.

MICHELLE OBAMA
ATTORNEY, AUTHOR, AND FORMER FIRST LADY OF THE UNITED STATES

My mom always told me to live with an open heart—when life gets tough, you should go out and help someone else.

JANE SEYMOUR

ENGLISH ACTRESS

I want to be *a* *fun*

mom. *Not* *a*

gasping-for-air *mom.*

MARISKA HARGITAY

AMERICAN ACTRESS

One of the things I learned the hard way was that it doesn't pay to get discouraged. Keeping busy and making optimism a way of life can restore your faith in yourself.

LUCILLE BALL
AMERICAN COMEDIAN, ACTRESS, AND MODEL

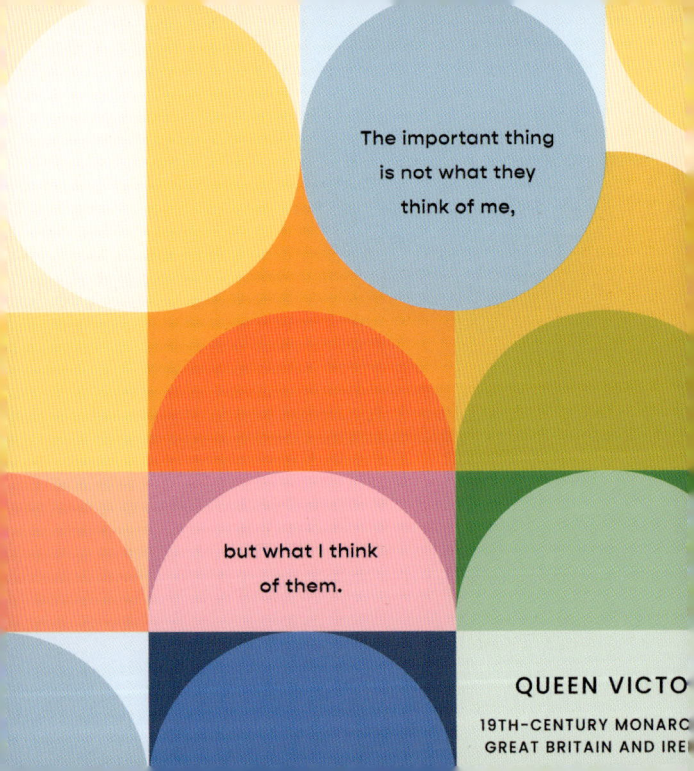

> The important thing is not what they think of me, but what I think of them.

QUEEN VICTO[RIA]

19TH-CENTURY MONARC[H OF]
GREAT BRITAIN AND IRE[LAND]

MY MOTHER TAUGHT ME ABOUT THE POWER OF INSPIRATION AND COURAGE, AND SHE DID IT WITH A STRENGTH AND A PASSION THAT I WISH COULD BE BOTTLED.

CARLY FIORINA

AMERICAN BUSINESSWOMAN, AUTHOR, AND POLITICIAN

Life excites me—just little, normal, everyday things. Getting out of bed. Getting dressed. Making food. I find it all exciting.

LIV TYL[ER]

AMERICAN ACTRESS AND MO[DEL]

I think there's a time to work, and everyone has to kind of adjust.

And then there's a time to relax, and be the mom or take the kids on vacation when you need to wind down.

So it's a matter of planning, and being able to map out your year or your week or let's start with the day.

It is just multi-tasking and being available.

VANESSA WILLIAMS
AMERICAN SINGER, ACTRESS, AND PRODUCER

ONLY MOTHERS CAN THINK OF THE FUTURE—

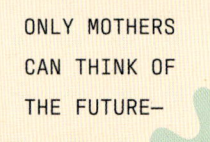

BECAUSE THEY GIVE BIRTH TO IT IN THEIR CHILDREN.

MAXIM GORKY
RUSSIAN WRITER AND POLITICAL ACTIVIST

PEOPLE ALWAYS ACCUSE ME OF BEING MOTIVATIONAL IN A WAY,

LIKE IT WAS A BAD THING,

BUT THAT'S JUST HOW I WAS RAISED.

MY MOM RAISED ME IN A POSITIVE ENVIRONMENT,

WITH LOTS OF LOVE IN MY HEART,

AND THAT REFLECTS IN MY MUSIC.

LENNY KRAVITZ
AMERICAN SINGER-SONGWRITER

I think it's worth trying to be a mother who delights in who her children are, in the knock-kn[ee] joke[s] and earnest questions. A mother who spends less time obsessing about w[hat] will hap[pen] or what has happened, and more time reveling in what is.

AYELET WALDMAN
ISRAELI-AMERICAN WRITER

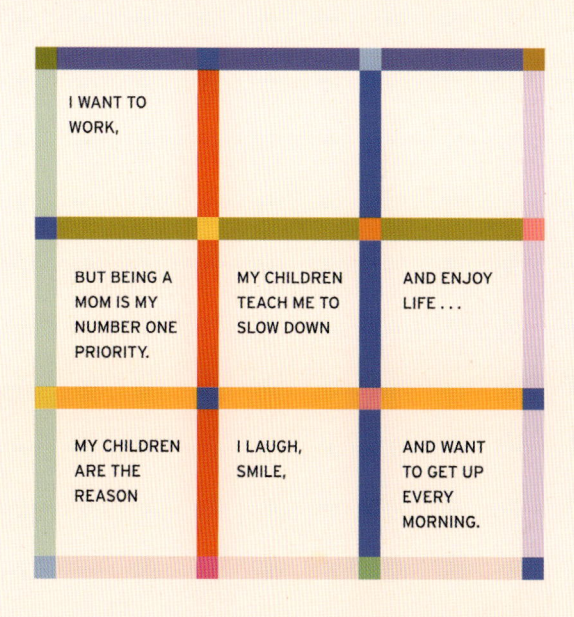

I WANT TO WORK, BUT BEING A MOM IS MY NUMBER ONE PRIORITY. MY CHILDREN TEACH ME TO SLOW DOWN AND ENJOY LIFE... MY CHILDREN ARE THE REASON I LAUGH, SMILE, AND WANT TO GET UP EVERY MORNING.

GENA LEE NOLIN

AMERICAN ACTRESS AND MODEL

Even a happy life
cannot be

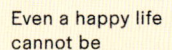

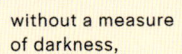

without a measure
of darkness,

and the word **happy**
would lose its meaning

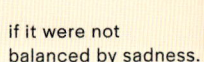

if it were not
balanced by sadness.

It is far better take things as they come
along with patience and equanimity.

CARL JUNG

SWISS PSYCHIATRIST AND THEORIST

I used to be obsessed with what other moms would do, but listening to your maternal instincts is always the right decision.

TORI SPELLING

AMERICAN ACTRESS AND AUTHOR

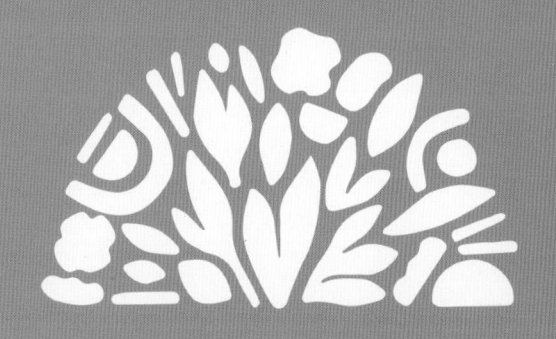

I love every second of being a mom.

LILY ALDRIDGE

AMERICAN MODEL

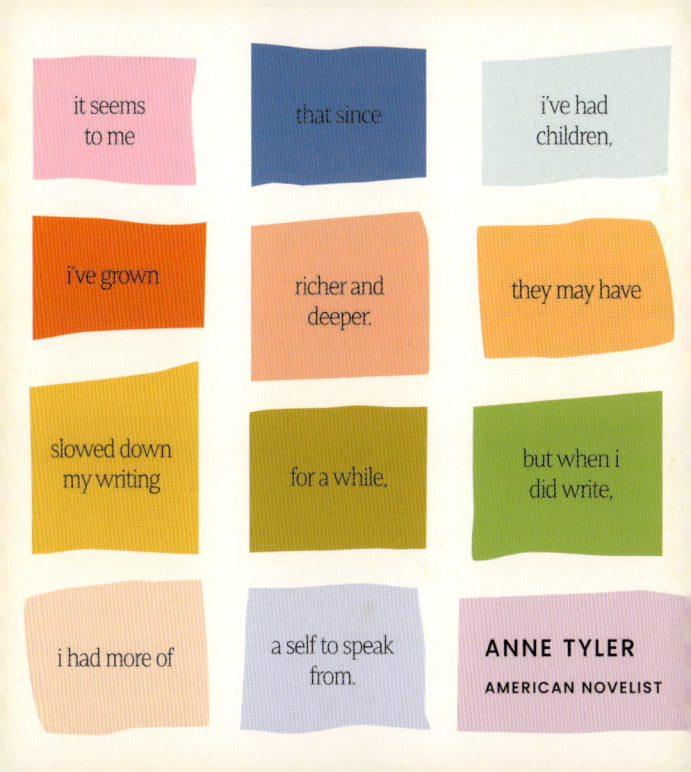

it seems to me that since i've had children, i've grown richer and deeper. they may have slowed down my writing for a while, but when i did write, i had more of a self to speak from.

ANNE TYLER
AMERICAN NOVELIST

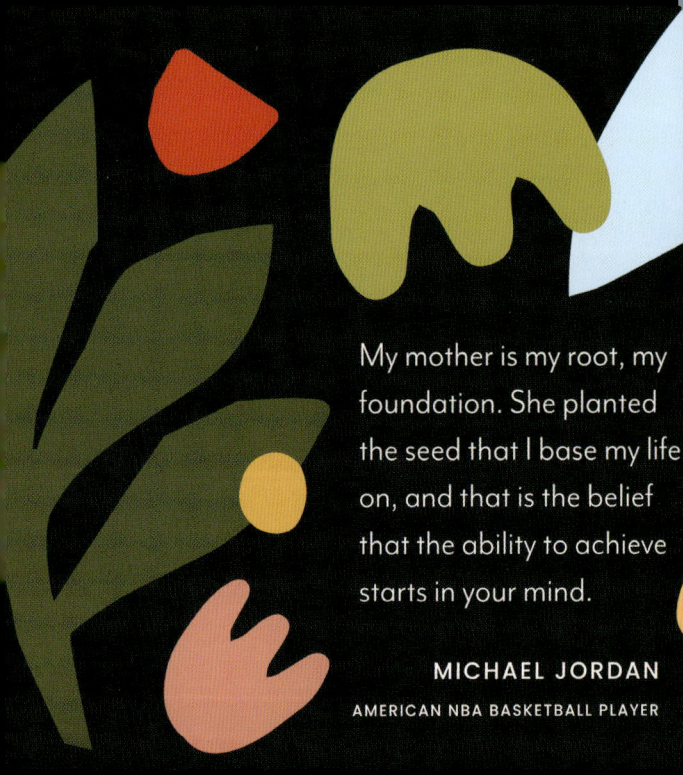

My mother is my root, my foundation. She planted the seed that I base my life on, and that is the belief that the ability to achieve starts in your mind.

MICHAEL JORDAN
AMERICAN NBA BASKETBALL PLAYER

Yes, Mother.

I can see you are flawed.

You have not hidden it.

That is your greatest gift to me.

ALICE WALKER
AMERICAN AUTHOR, POET, AND SOCIAL ACTIVIST

SELFLESSNESS

If you're a mom, you're a superhero.

Period.

ROSIE POPE
BRITISH-AMERICAN ENTREPRENEUR AND BUSINESSWOMAN

The natural state of motherhood is unselfishness. When you become a mother, you are no longer the center of your own universe. You relinquish that position to your children

JESSICA LANGE

AMERICAN ACTRESS

> A mother is a person who, seeing there are only four pieces of pie for five people, promptly announces she never did care for pie.

TENNEVA JORDAN
AMERICAN AUTHOR

Love is a fruit in season at all times and within the reach of every hand.

MOTHER TERESA

ALBANIAN-BORN INDIAN CATHOLIC NUN
AND HUMANITARIAN

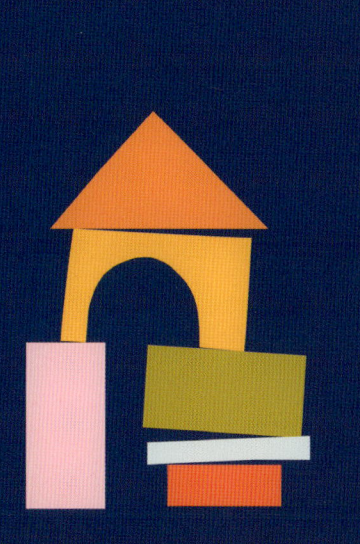

A mother never quite leaves her children at home, even when she doesn't take them along.

MARGARET CULKIN BANNING

AMERICAN AUTHOR AND SOCIAL ACTIVIST

Making the decision to have a child is momentous. It is to decide forever to have your heart go walking around outside your body.

ELIZABETH STONE

AMERICAN AUTHOR AND HISTORIAN

BECOMING A MOTHER MAKES YOU THE MOTHER OF ALL CHILDREN. FROM NOW ON, EACH WOUNDED, ABANDONED, FRIGHTENED CHILD IS YOURS. YOU LIVE IN THE SUFFERING MOTHERS OF EVERY RACE AND CREED AND WEEP WITH THEM. YOU LONG TO COMFORT ALL WHO ARE DESOLATE.

CHARLOTTE GRAY

ENGLISH-BORN CANADIAN AUTHOR

MORE THAN IN ANY OTHER
HUMAN RELATIONSHIP,

OVERWHELMINGLY MORE,
MOTHERHOOD MEANS

BEING INSTANTLY
INTERRUPTIBLE, RESPONSIVE,
AND RESPONSIBLE.

TILLIE OLS
AMERICAN WRITER AND FEMINIST LEA

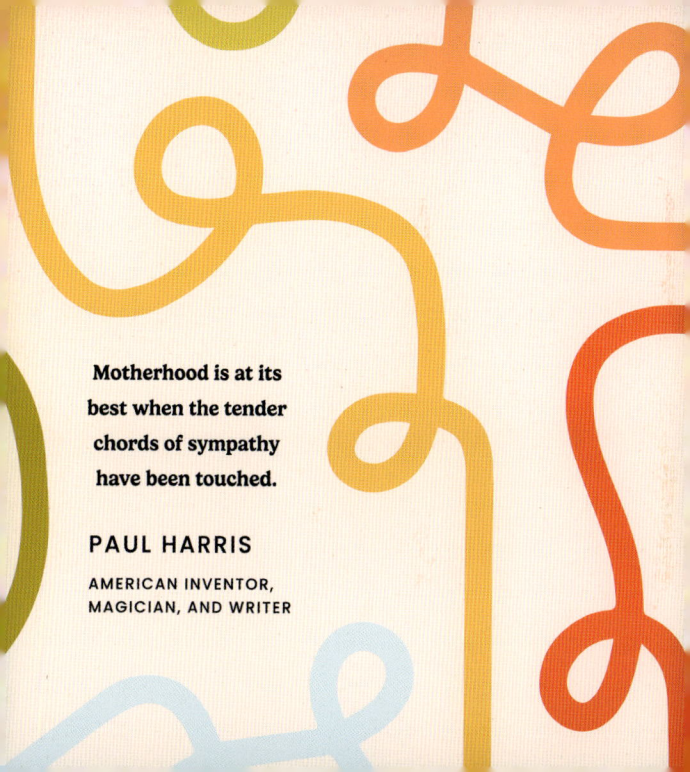

Motherhood is at its best when the tender chords of sympathy have been touched.

PAUL HARRIS

AMERICAN INVENTOR, MAGICIAN, AND WRITER

When you are a mother, you are never really alone in your thoughts. A mother always has to think twice, once for herself and once for her child.

SOPHIA LOREN

ITALIAN ACTRESS

Motherhood is the biggest gamble in the world. It is the glorious life force. It's huge and scary—it's an act of infinite optimism.

GILDA RADNER
AMERICAN ACTRESS AND COMEDIAN

BEING A SINGER IS ALL ABOUT ME. ABOUT EGO.

BEING A MOM IS ALL ABOUT BEING SELFLESS

—TWO DIFFERENT WORLDS.

GWEN STEFANI
AMERICAN SINGER-SONGWRITER

Man can never
be a woman's
equal

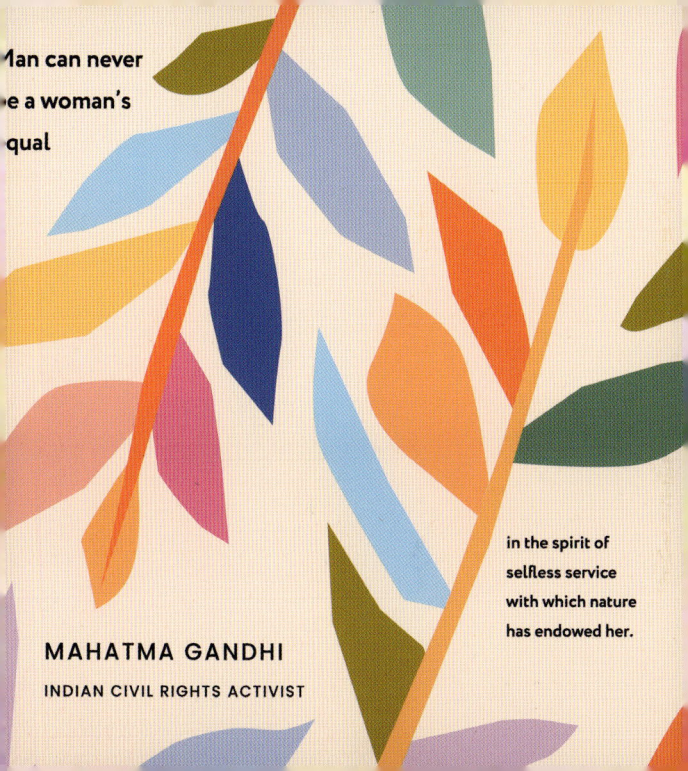

in the spirit of
selfless service
with which nature
has endowed her.

MAHATMA GANDHI
INDIAN CIVIL RIGHTS ACTIVIST

My mom and I have always been very close. She is my best friend.

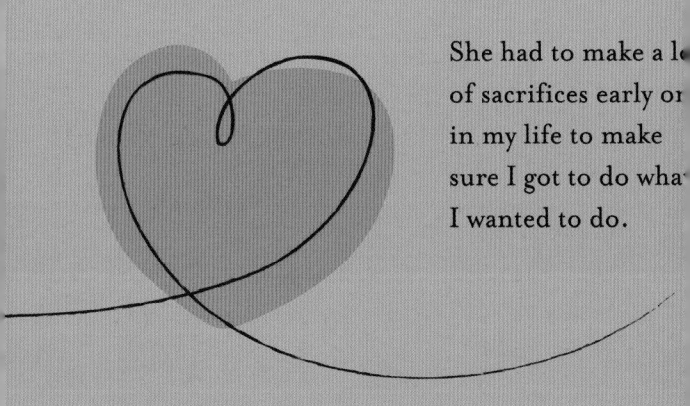

She had to make a lot of sacrifices early on in my life to make sure I got to do what I wanted to do.

NORAH JONES
AMERICAN SINGER-SONGWRITER AND ACTRESS

The passion of love is essentially selfish, while motherhood widens the circle of our feelings.

HONORÉ DE BALZAC
FRENCH NOVELIST AND PLAYWRIGHT

> My mother taught me how to love.
>
> My mom is the most loving person I know.
>
> **CHANNING TATUM**
> AMERICAN ACTOR AND PRODUC[ER]

A MOTHER'S LOVE
HAS THE ABILITY
TO FORGIVE EVEN
THE MOST
DIFFICULT CHILD.

ANONYMOUS

You are a miracle. And I have to love you this fiercely: so that you can feel it even after you leave for school, or even while you are asleep, or even after your childhood becomes a memory. You'll forget all this when you grow up. But it's okay. Being a mother means having your heart broken. And it means loving and losing and falling apart and coming back together.

KATHERINE CENTER

AMERICAN AUTHOR

Giving kids clothes and food is one of thing, but it's much more important to teach them that other people besides themselves are important and that the best thing they can do with their lives is to use them in the service of other people.

DOLORES HUERTA

AMERICAN LABOR LEADER AND CIVIL RIGHTS ACTIVIST

It takes someone really brave to be a mother, someone strong to raise a child, and someone special to love someone more than herself.

RITU GHATOUREY
INDIAN-AMERICAN AUTHOR

PERSEVERANCE

Being a mom has made me so tired. And so happy.

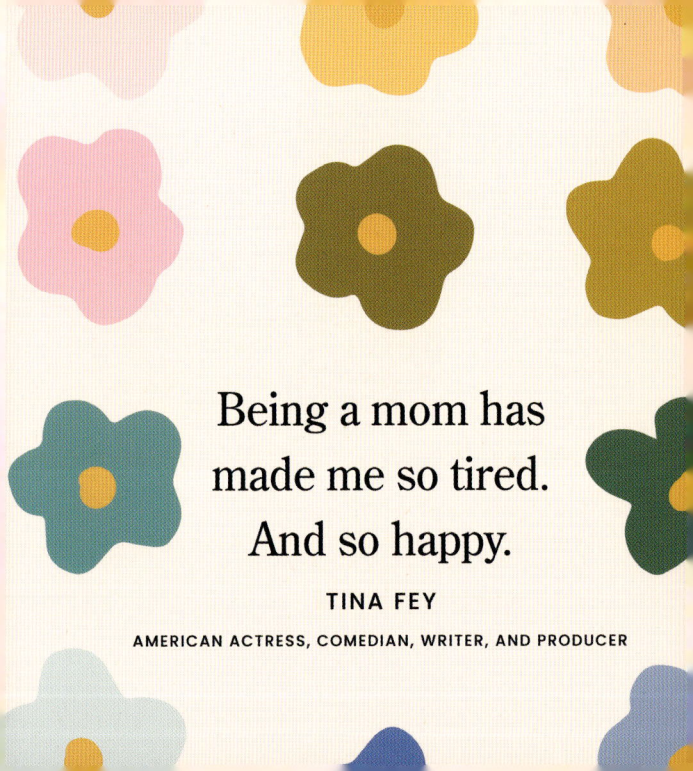

TINA FEY

AMERICAN ACTRESS, COMEDIAN, WRITER, AND PRODUCER

MOTHER IS A VERB, NOT A NOUN

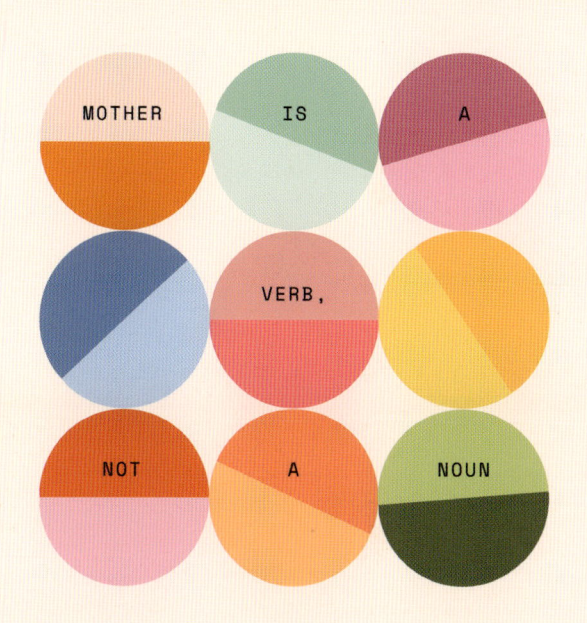

ERMA BOMBECK

AMERICAN AUTHOR AND HUMORIST

Motherhood brings as much joy as ever, but it still brings boredom, exhaustion, and sorrow, too. Nothing else ever will make you as happy or as sad, as proud or as tired, for nothing is quite as hard as helping a person develop his own individuality, especially while you struggle to keep your own.

MARGUERITE KELLY AND ELIA PARSONS
THE MOTHER'S ALMANAC

> As a mom, I know that raising children is the hardest job there is.

HILARY ROSEN

AMERICAN LOBBYIST AND POLITICAL PUNDIT

MOTHERHOOD IS THE GREATEST THING AND THE HARDEST THING.

RICKI LAKE
AMERICAN ACTRESS,
PRODUCER,
AND TV HOST

I believe this with all my heart: the greatest coach of all time in my eyes is my mom. She's instilled in me a toughness and a perseverance and just a never-quit mentality, and I thank her every day for providing that for me, for what she sacrificed her life for.

SCOTT BROOKS

AMERICAN NBA BASKETBALL PLAYER AND COACH

THE PHRASE "WORKING MOTHER" IS REDUNDANT.

JANE SELLMAN

AMERICAN AUTHOR AND PROFESSOR

Having kids—the responsibility of rearing good, ethical, responsible human beings—is the biggest job anyone can embark on.

MARIA SHRIVER
AMERICAN AUTHOR AND JOURNALIST

Nothing that doesn't push you past your limits can change your life. It's true of work, it's true of parenting, and it's true—a hundred times over—of love.

KATHERINE CENTER

NOTHING WORTHWHILE IS EVER EASY

SUCCESS
———

Men are what their mothers made them

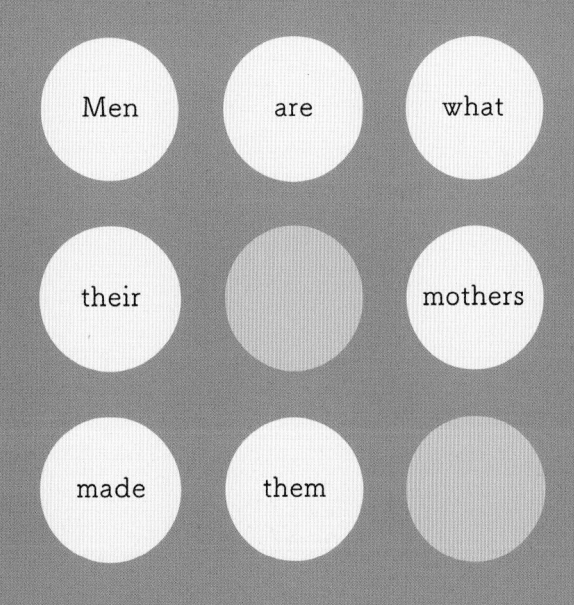

RALPH WALDO EMERSON
AMERICAN TRANSCENDENTALIST WRITER

All that I am, or hope to be, I owe to my angel mother.

ABRAHAM LINCOLN

16TH US PRESIDENT

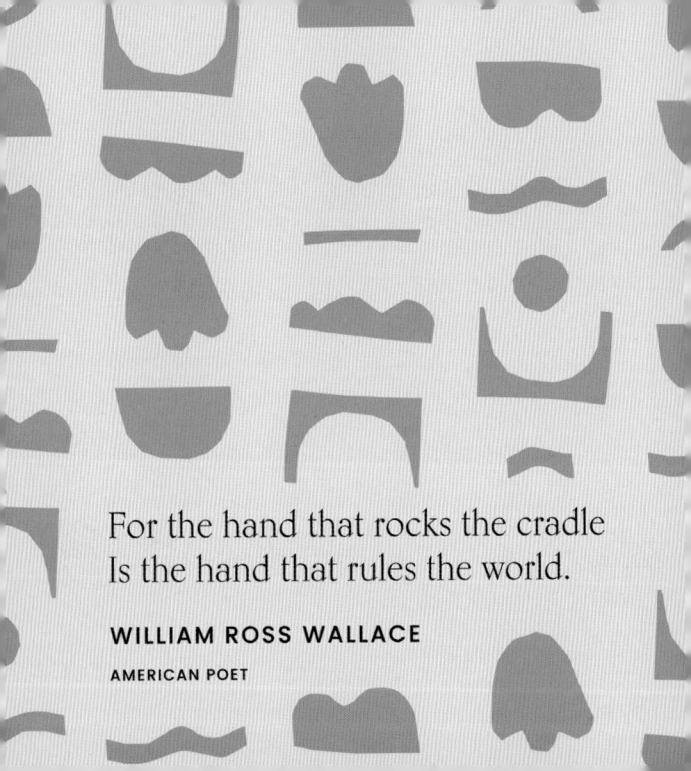

For the hand that rocks the cradle
Is the hand that rules the world.

WILLIAM ROSS WALLACE

AMERICAN POET

I'M A MOM FIRST, A SINGER SECOND.

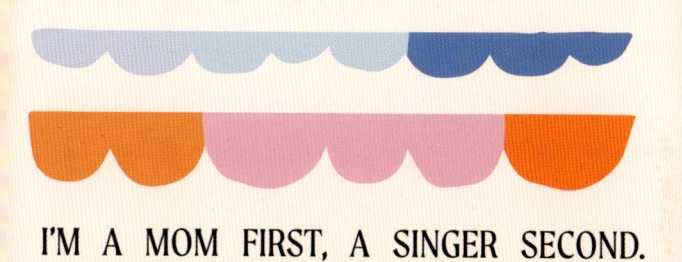

GRETCHEN WILSON

AMERICAN COUNTRY MUSIC ARTIST

> *As far as I'm concerned, there's no job more important on the planet than being a mom.*

MARK WAHLBERG

AMERICAN ACTOR

My mother was the most beautiful woman I ever saw. All I am I owe to my mother. I attribute all my success in life to the moral, intellectual, and physical education I received from her.

GEORGE WASHINGTON

1ST US PRESIDENT

> I always tell people, I'm a better swimmer because I'm a mom and a better mom because I'm a swimmer.

AMANDA BEARD

AMERICAN OLYMPIC SWIMMER

WOMEN DO NOT HAVE TO SACRIFICE PERSONHOOD IF THEY ARE MOTHERS. THEY DO NOT HAVE TO SACRIFICE MOTHERHOOD IN ORDER TO BE PERSONS. LIBERATION WAS MEANT TO EXPAND WOMEN'S OPPORTUNITIES, NOT TO LIMIT THEM. THE SELF-ESTEEM THAT HAS BEEN FOUND IN NEW PURSUITS CAN ALSO BE FOUND IN MOTHERING.

ELAINE HEFFNER
AMERICAN PSYCHOTHERAPIST, AUTHOR, AND EDUCATOR

> OF ALL THE ROLES I'VE PLAYED,
>
> NONE HAS BEEN AS FULFILLING
>
> AS BEING A MOTHER.

ANNETTE FUNICELLO
AMERICAN ACTRESS AND SINGER

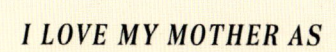

I LOVE MY MOTHER AS THE TREES LOVE WATER AND SUNSHINE—SHE HELPS ME GROW, PROSPER, AND REACH GREAT HEIGHTS.

TERRI GUILLEMETS
AMERICAN ANTHOLOGIST

> IT IS NOT WHAT YOU DO FOR YOUR CHILDREN, BUT WHAT YOU HAVE TAUGHT THEM TO DO FOR THEMSELVES, THAT WILL MAKE THEM SUCCESSFUL HUMAN BEINGS.

ANN LANDERS
AMERICAN ADVICE COLUMNIST

The mother is the most precious possession of the nation, so precious that society advances its highest well-being when it protects the functions of the mother.

ELLEN KEY

SWEDISH WRITER

I REGARD NO MAN AS POOR WHO HAS A GODLY MOTHER

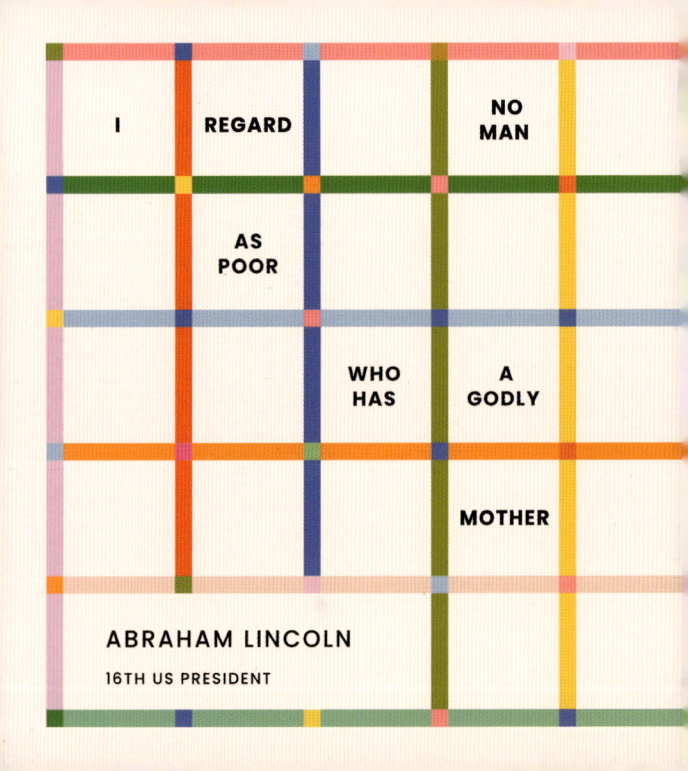

ABRAHAM LINCOLN
16TH US PRESIDENT

> I looked on child-rearing not only as a work of love and duty but as a profession that was fully as interesting and challenging as any honorable profession in the world and one that demanded the best I could bring to it.

ROSE KENNEDY

AMERICAN PHILANTHROPIST
AND MOTHER OF PRESIDENT JOHN F. KENNEDY

LEARNING

> THE MOTHER'S HEART IS THE CHILD'S SCHOOLROOM.

HENRY WARD BEECHER
AMERICAN CLERGYMAN AND SOCIAL REFORMER

THE BEST ACADEMY, THE MOTHER'S KNEE.

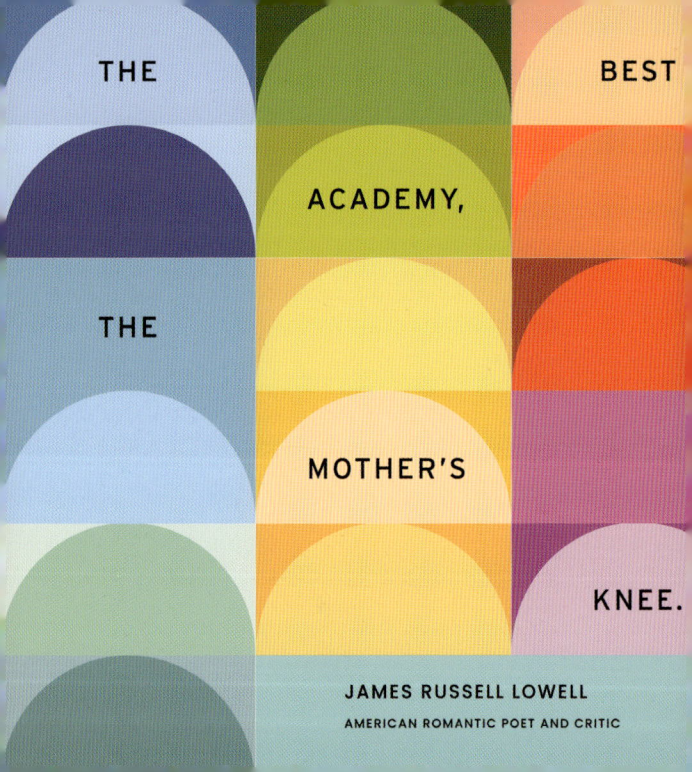

JAMES RUSSELL LOWELL
AMERICAN ROMANTIC POET AND CRITIC

I know how to do anything; I'm a mom.

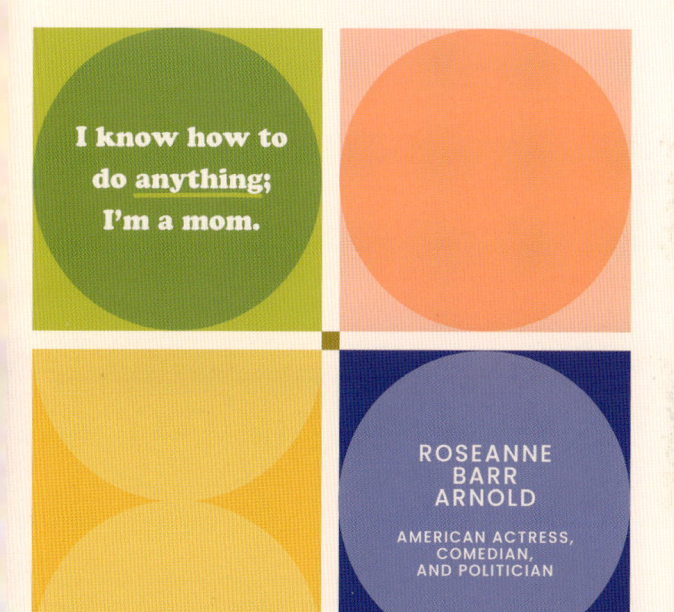

ROSEANNE BARR ARNOLD

AMERICAN ACTRESS, COMEDIAN, AND POLITICIAN

The art of mothering is to teach the art of living to children.

ELAINE HEFFNER
AMERICAN PSYCHOTHERAPIST, AUTHOR, AND EDUCATOR

WISDOM

AND

COMPASSION

IT IS NOT UNTIL YOU BECOME A MOTHER THAT YOUR JUDGMENT SLOWLY TURNS TO COMPASSION AND UNDERSTANDING ♥

ERMA BOMBECK

AMERICAN AUTHOR AND HUMORIST

Most mothers are instinctive philosophers.

HARRIET BEECHER STOWE

AMERICAN AUTHOR AND ABOLITIONIST

WHAT DO GIRLS DO WHO HAVEN'T ANY MOTHERS TO HELP THEM THROUGH THEIR TROUBLES?

LOUISA MAY ALCOTT

AMERICAN NOVELIST

Motherhood has a very humanizing effect. Everything gets reduced to essentials.

MERYL STREEP

AMERICAN ACTRESS

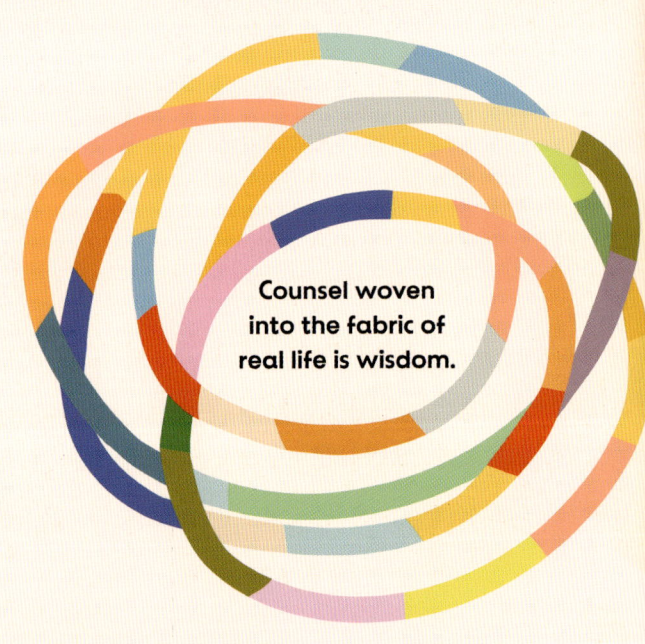

> Counsel woven into the fabric of real life is wisdom.

WALTER BENJAMIN

GERMAN LITERARY CRITIC AND PHILOSOPHER

I am sure that if the mothers of various nations could meet, there would be no more wars.

E. M. FORSTER

ENGLISH NOVELIST AND WRITER

A mother understands what a child does not say.

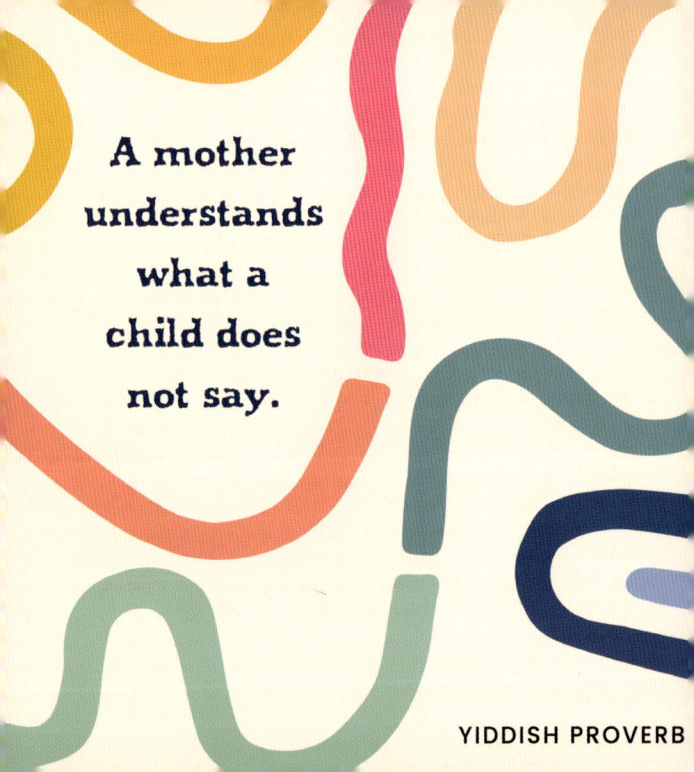

YIDDISH PROVERB

A mother knows what her child's gone through, even if she didn't see it herself.

PRAMOEDYA ANANTA TOER
INDONESIAN AUTHOR AND HISTORIAN

SPIRITUALITY

Heaven is at the feet of mothers.

ARABIC PROVERB

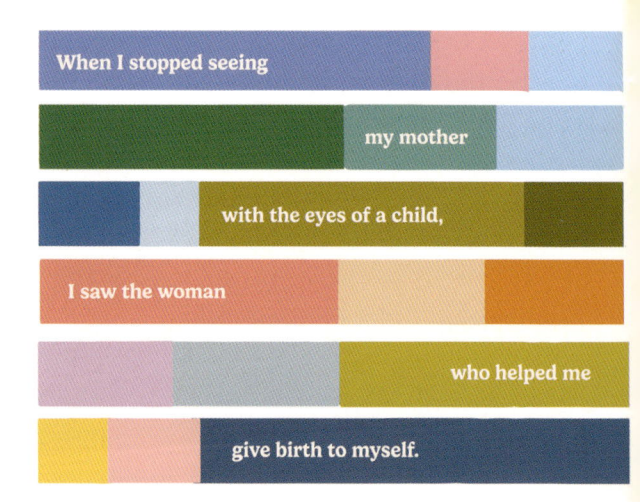

> When I stopped seeing my mother with the eyes of a child, I saw the woman who helped me give birth to myself.

NANCY FRIDAY

AMERICAN AUTHOR

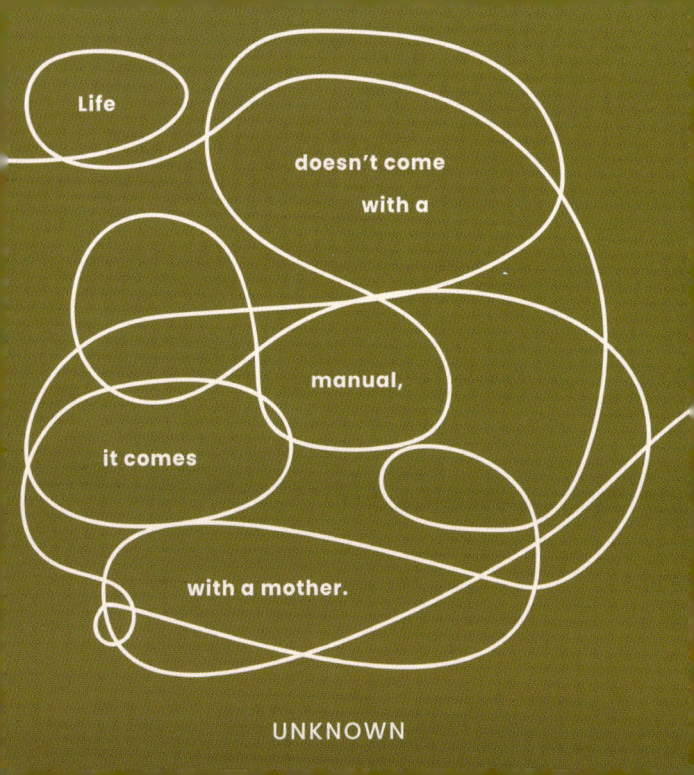

Life doesn't come with a manual, it comes with a mother.

UNKNOWN

God could not be everywhere, so he made mothers.

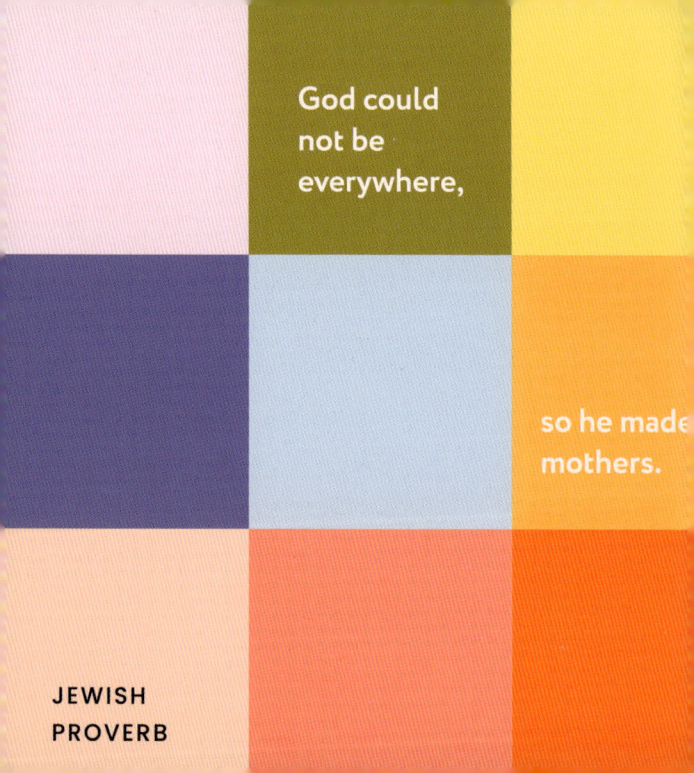

JEWISH PROVERB

The heart of a mother is a deep abyss at the bottom of which you will always find forgiveness.

HONORÉ DE BALZAC FRENCH NOVELIST AND PLAYWRIGHT

I believe the choice to become a mother is the choice to become one of the greatest spiritual teachers there is.

OPRAH WINFREY
AMERICAN TV PERSONALITY AND ACT

About the Designer

Olivia Herrick is a graphic designer based in the Twin Cities of Minnesota, best known for her playful, vibrant, and positive artwork. Though you will often find her glued to her computer at her studio, Olivia finds her greatest inspiration in the great outdoors. Follow her and her work @oliviaherrickdesign.

About Familius

Visit Our Website: www.familius.com

Familius is a global trade publishing company that publishes books and other content to help families be happy. We believe that happy families are key to a better society and the foundation of a happy life. The greatest work anyone will ever do will be within the walls of his or her own home. And we don't mean vacuuming! We recognize that every family looks different and passionately believe in helping all families find greater joy, whatever their situation. To that end, we publish beautiful books that help families live our 10 Habits of Happy Family Life: *love together, play together, learn together, work together, talk together, heal together, read together, eat together, give together,* and *laugh together.* Further, Familius does not discriminate on the basis of race, color, religion, gender, age, nationality, disability, caste, or sexual orientation in any of its activities or operations. Founded in 2012, Familius is located in Sanger, California.

Connect

Facebook: www.facebook.com/familiusbooks
Pinterest: www.pinterest.com/familiusbooks
Instagram: @FamiliusBooks
TikTok: @FamiliusBooks

*The most important work you ever do will
be within the walls of your own home.*